Awaken Within

Mandalachakra™

A journey to your soul

Awaken Within - Mandalachakra™ - A Journey to your Soul
Author: Laural Virtues Wauters
Artist: Laural Virtues Wauters
Publisher: Seven Earthly Virtues, LLC

For more information visit:
www.mandalachakra.com or www.treeoflifeawakening.com

"Come out of the circle of time .
And into the circle of love."
- Rumi -

Table of Contents

"The first peace,
which is the most important,
is that which comes within the souls of people
when they realize their relationship their oneness
with the universe and all its powers,
and when they realize
that at the center of the universe
dwells the Great Spirit,
and that this center
is really everywhere,
it is within each of us."
- Black Elk -

Laural Virtues Wauters – is a mandala facilitator, artist, shaman and soul coach. Laural gently encourages you to begin the sacred journey of awakening within. This inner and outer journey is one that facilitates deep emotional healing by understanding the stories you hold and their influence on your conscious and unconscious mind. By awakening your soul, you begin to see how to heal your self and your world.

Laural is a certified mandala facilitator through Dr. Rajita Sivananda (Judith Cornell Ph.D.) Author of the award-winning books: MANDALA: Luminous Symbols for Healing. The Mandala Healing Kit, Amma: Healing the Heart of the World and Drawing the Light from Within. Laural is also a graduate of the Four Winds - Healing the Light Body School of Energy Medicine founded by Dr. Alberto Villoldo. Dr. Villoldo is the best-selling author of several books including Shaman, Healer, Sage, Yoga, Power and Sprit, The Four Insights. Laural wrote and self-published her autobiography, The Guardian Tree and currently teaches classes and retreats.

To learn more or to order the companion card deck visit:
www.mandalachakra.com

Mandala – The Sacred Circle

Mandala is the Sanskirt word for sacred circle. Mankind has always associated the circle as a symbol of creation and the great cycles of life. They saw the circle as a sacred gateway to their inner most knowing as well as the ever-expanding universe. The mandala is a tool that helps to make the invisible visible and the unknown known. The great mysteries of life are revealed within it if we allow ourselves to be open.

Chakra – The Sacred Wheel

Chakra is the Sanskrit word for sacred wheel. Over 3000 years ago devout Yogis sensed invisible wheels of energy within their physical body. Yoga means to "Yoke with Spirit", and a Yogi is someone who commits their life to this practice. Through deep meditation these Yogis could feel that these subtle wheels were related to 7 specific areas within their body. They named these wheels Chakras as each one resonated to a different vibration. From these vibrations they created mantras or vocal sounds that improved the flow of energy within each chakra. These mantras helped them awaken to higher levels of consciousness, ultimately becoming one with spirit. Mantras evolved through the creation of yantras and mandalas as another way to awaken.

Mandalachakra™

By sensing the expansive energy of the mandala within each chakra you awaken the conscious and unconscious self. Awakening within helps you feel connected to your physical and soul body. Healing at the level of the soul empowers your life force as you see the unlimited potential within you.

Awaken Within

Fiftyone hand drawn mandalas have been specially designed to guide you through the seven chakras of your physical body within the seven levels of perception of your soul body. Each mandala chakra is paired with information and insights to guide you on the journey of awakening within.

Learning about your chakras within each of these perceptual states will help you gain a broader understanding of the body, mind and soul connection. By seeing yourself as a soul within a human body you awaken within. From this place you realize you are both human and divine. This is symbolic of awakening the Tree of Life Within as the Tree of Knowledge helps you reclaim your true nature. You are no longer separated from yourself, or your source, for you are one.

Seven chakras of the physical body
Root – Muscular/Skeletal & Excretory System
Sacral – Reproductive System
Solar Plexus – Digestive, Lymphatic & Immune System
Heart – Circulatory & Respiratory System
Throat – Endocrine & Vocal System
Third Eye – Nervous & Sensory System
Crown – Belief System

Seven levels of perception of the soul body
Physical – Messengers of Nature
Symbolic – Sacred Geometry
Mythic – Elements of Nature
Energetic – Chakras of our Energy Body
Sacred – Stories of Belief
Consciousness – Awakening Within
Soul – The Infinite One

" *It became increasingly plain to me that the mandala is the path to the centre, to individuation. I knew that in finding the mandala as an expression of the self I had attained what was for me the ultimate.* "

- C. G. Jung -

Awakening the Collective Unconscious

Carl Jung, (1875 – 1961) a Swiss psychologist, founded analytical psychology and the concept of individuation. His focus was on integrating the opposite aspects of the conscious and unconscious mind to deepen the sense of self. He felt that the human psyche was "by nature religious" and that the mystical heart was at the core of all belief. To heal the soul would require a journey within to meet the self and the divine at the same time. Jung saw the world from the archetypal level of the collective unconscious. By awakening the unconscious mind we become conscious of our soul. When we become conscious of our soul we can begin to awaken the collective unconscious by consciously healing our world. When we see our self as one...we awaken to all.

"A human being is a part of the whole
called by us "the universe,"
a part limited in time and space.
He experiences himself
his thoughts and feelings,
as something separate from the rest
a kind of optical delusion of his consciousness.
This delusion is a kind of prison,
restricting our personal desires and affections. Our task
must be to free ourselves from this prison by
widening our circle of
understanding and compassion
to embrace all living creatures
and the whole of nature in its beauty."
- Albert Einstein -

Mandala Chakras – At a Glance

The above mandalas represent the seven chakras in each of the seven perceptual states. The bottom row represents the root chakra; the top row represents the crown chakra.

The mandalas in this book are drawn on black paper. Black represents our un-manifested self, the dark matter of the universe filled with unlimited potential. These mandalas are designed to help you see the beauty and the possibility that awaits you in both the darkness and the light.

Physical
Messengers of Nature

The connection between nature and man has been understood since the dawn of Homo sapiens in Africa over 200,000 years ago. When man saw rainbows after a rainstorm they interpreted them as benevolent Serpents in the sky. Early shamans or sages became the visionaries; the medicine men and women who helped their tribe interpret these signs from nature. They had the ability to sense the energy of the land, plants and animals. They knew how to read the stars and connect with the directions of the wind. They were able to use these insights to guide their tribes out of Africa and populate the world. As mankind encountered new animals and plants they learned from them. They saw that plants and animals held knowledge just as their ancestors did. They believed in contacting these ancestor spirits for guidance and assistance during hard times. This gave them the ability to bring new insights to their life or to identify healing herbs for certain illnesses. Many cultures saw trees as a way to travel to the past, present or the future. Trees were seen as gateways to other worlds. Shamans understood that everything was interconnected and interdependent, they taught the importance of honoring all aspects of life, death, birth and rebirth. Everything from stones, animals, trees, water was seen as sacred and were honored for their gifts.

"In the beginning of all things,
wisdom and knowledge
were with the animals."
- Pawnee Chief -

1. Serpent - South - Root

The Serpent of Light is wrapped around your root chakra encouraging you to release what holds you. As you trust the process of releasing and receiving nourishment from the earth you create a loving and reciprocal relationship. Just as the serpent sheds its skin you must learn to shed the limiting beliefs and clutter in your life so you can move forward with more ease. Imagine that you are awakening the Serpent of Light within your root chakra. Visualize the serpent of light traveling through your energy body to help you shed what no longer serves you. Serpent shows you how to move through this world with beauty and grace by gliding effortlessly through life. Located at the base of your spine, the root chakra serves as your direct connection to the Earth and what a gift it is to be human. Serpents and humans have been intertwined since the beginning of time. Once seen as a sacred being that lived in the sky it has also become associated with temptation, division and original sin on earth.

In Abrahamic belief (Judaism, Christianity and Islam) the serpent is held responsible for tempting Eve to eat of the Tree of Knowledge. For this act Adam and Eve are forbidden to eat of the Tree of Life and cast out of the Garden of Eden. This story holds the archetypal wound of original sin and the loss of innocence. In it we lose our memory of being both human and divine. It is no coincidence that Serpent is the first chakra mandala on this journey of awakening within. To make peace with Serpent opens the door to making peace within your self. The Ouroborus is an ancient symbol of a serpent eating its tail. It thereby creates a circular and infinite world. By dying to its old self, it is able to nourish itself with the wisdom of what it has shed so it can rebirth itself over and over again. Plato saw the Ouroborus as the first living thing in the universe. Yogis saw it as the mothering Kundalini energy of divine power. Meso-Americans saw it as Quetzalcoatl the benevolent serpent God that lived in the center of the Milky Way. Carl Jung saw the Ouroborus as the Archetype for the human psyche and alchemy. Ningishzita is the Sumerian Serpent God of medicine, translated as "lord of the good tree". The Greek God of medicine, Asclepius, held a staff with a sacred single serpent coiled around a rough-hewn knotty tree limb, symbolizing renewal of youth as the serpent casts off its skin. The Gods Mercury and Hermes were associated with the creation of the Caduceus, a wooden rod entwined by two serpents topped with a pair of wings. This image is still used today to symbolize modern medicine. The rod represents our spinal column or the Tree of Life. The serpents represent the male and female aspects of our self and the dual strands of our DNA. When you see that you are intertwined within yourself as male and female, human and divine, heaven and earth you can release the limited belief that you are separate or alone. Reclaim your souls unlimited potential and embrace the beauty and grace within you.

18

2. Jaguar - West - Sacral

Jaguar is the peaceful warrior who reminds you of your inner wisdom and power. Jaguar teaches you to use your power wisely by stepping out of judgment and giving you the strength to look deep within your shadows. If you do not look at those things that scare you, you increase your risk of abusing your power towards yourself or others. By looking at what you fear and understanding that the opposite of what you see is your truth, you can begin to step out of judgment and live in that truth. Jaguar helps you to see that your fears are being fed by a wounded part of you or a limiting belief you are hanging onto. Instead you must feed yourself love and compassion. As you look deep within the darkness of your own shadows you can retrieve the insights that are waiting for you. From this place you can heal from within. Begin to see that your true power is to be at peace within yourself and your world. Jaguar encourages you to go into the darkness and claim the wisdom to be a person of peaceful power.

When you use your power wisely you are able to speak your truth and actively practice peace. This is the way of the Jaguar, the Peaceful Warrior that resides within you. Located within the area of your reproductive system, the sacral chakra represents your passion as well as your creative and sexual power. This power within us can be frightening if we do not know how to use it wisely. It is important to learn how to balance your power by stepping out of judgment. The Jaguar is a warm-blooded mammal that sees through the dark. This gives them the ability to hunt at night when many other animals or birds are resting. They also represent the top of the food chain within Meso-America. In North America and Europe it is Panther or Wolf, in Asia and Africa they are Lions and Tigers. Together they represent the dynamic relationship of predator prey. Within our energy body this can trigger our flight, fight or freeze response and is closely associated with healing your inner Jaguar. Jaguars hunt to survive and spend most of their time lying peacefully within the trees of the rainforest. They hold no judgment of right or wrong, dark or light, black or white. As the Sunsets each evening Jaguar encourages us to enter the world of darkness, as it is important and necessary. The darkness gives us a place to rest, recharge and to dream. If you are having nightmares it is your brains way of working through your fears. Jaguar is reminding you to step out of judgment of what frightens you. By bringing these fears forward and out of the shadows you can begin to see them for what they are. Most of the time they are triggered by events of the day, old wounds of your childhood or stories you have learned from your ancestors. When you see that your dreams hold insights for you, you can reclaim the gifts they bring. Now is a good time to journal your dreams. Call on the energy of Jaguar to help you go into the darkness and see what is truly waiting for you. Journal your dreams and see the insights they hold.

3. Hummingbird - North - Solar Plexus

Hummingbird helps you reconnect with the sweetness and joy in your life. If your life has been traumatic or hectic try to slow down and rest for a while. Even hummingbirds perch on branches to rest and watch the world around them. Take time to nourish your self with healthy food, love and compassion. If you are feeling disconnected, call on Hummingbird to help you retrieve parts of yourself that feel lost. Soul loss is caused by trauma, grief and other life experiences. As we lose parts of our soul we can begin to feel less whole, which can lead to depression or anxiety. If you are feeling lost call on Hummingbird to help you retrieve those parts of yourself. Imagine a luminous thread that connects you to these parts of your soul that are feeling afraid, unloved or lonely. Travel along that thread and listen to what your soul is asking for. Honor and heal the inner child within you that needs to feel loved unconditionally, now and forever. Bring this healed part of your soul into your heart.

Enjoy the sweetness of your life as you begin to live from a place of gratitude. Hummingbird helps you see life as a sacred fairytale. It is a reminder that what seems impossible is possible. Ask for Hummingbird's guidance to help you rewrite the stories that may be holding you from moving forward. Hummingbird inspires you to live in a place of constant gratitude. Be grateful for the most the difficult times of your life by seeing the lessons and wisdom they gave you. Each of them holds an insight that provides fuel for your journey. This fuel ingnites our soul and reminds us that we are alive and able to see life from this new place. The energy of Hummingbird is located in the solar plexus or stomach area of your body. It represents the eternal light that shines within you and the internal source that fuels you. Scientists are still trying to understand how the Hummingbird is able to travel such long distances twice a year without stopping to recharge. Their journey is a mythic journey as it takes on mythical proportations. Hummingbirds are courageous and sweet reminders that your life is also a mythical journey. Hummingbird shows us that it time to lighten the load you are carrying and to bring enchantment back into your life. The energy of a Hummingbird can also be seen in Dragonflies and Butterflies or mythical creatures such as Dragons and Unicorns. Remember that the impossible is possible. Now is a good time to do something sweet just for you. Bring flowers into your life to remind you of hummingbird. Reconnect with people, places or things that bring you joy. Let the child within you be heard as you see your life with wonder. Feel the beauty in everything and everyone and allow it to be reflected within you.

4. Eagle - East - Heart

Eagle is appearing to you now to help you see the bigger picture of your life. Eagle is asking you to see with your heart instead of your eyes and to allow your heart to open to accepting unconditional love. If your heart feels heavy ask Eagle to carry you above the stories, above the wounds where you can feel as if you are flying on currents of pure love. From this place know that you have the choice to release the stories that you are holding. Allow your heart to open to ultimate compassion, forgiveness and love. Connect with your true nature, as Eagle wants you to see that you are from the earth and also from the stars. Eagle gives you the ability to dream consciously and make those dreams a reality. Envision your past, present and future as one big dream that is carrying you forward into what you want to become. Don't be afraid to dream big for Eagle allows you to open your hearts to all possibilities. The energy of Eagle resides in our heart and is the anchor point within our body.

It unites our earthly body with our soul body. The Eagle is often seen as the largest bird that soars wing tip to wing tip between the heavens and the earth. For this reason the Eagle carries the essence of pure energy. As the Sun rises to signal a new day the eagle reminds us that we can fly above the stories that hold us. We can travel to a higher place where we gain a new perspective and see with new eyes. We can see the bigger picture of our lives yet still see all the details. From this place we see our stories for what they are, and can choose to fly above them versus staying engaged or held by them. The Eagle reminds us to soar with our hearts wide open as if our arms are stretched as far as they can reach on both sides. When we soar on the currents of pure energy we feel free to be who we truly are. Nothing defines you, nothing holds you, and you just are. Eagle is the ultimate symbol of freedom. There is a story of when Eagle and Condor will fly wing tip to wing tip in harmony, bringing balance between the worlds of the Southern and Northern hemispheres. This will signal the time to come. The truth is that the time to come is now. Eagle acts as a bridge between our lower three-earthly/human chakras and our upper three-divine/ethereal chakras. Eagle reminds us that our true nature is both human and divine and that this knowing resides in our hearts. The Eagle is also the bird of the East, the direction of the rising Sun. It has been symbolic of a new dawn for civilizations throughout the world. Within many beliefs systems the direction of East is the most sacred as it marks the rebirth or return of the Sun each day. Eagle is the bringer of that light within you. See with new eyes the potential of each new day and a new beginning. When you embrace the energy of Eagle you fly above the mundane and into the expansiveness of your unlimited self. When you see your life from this perspective you can free your soul and float above your stories. Take the time to soar and look at life with new eyes.

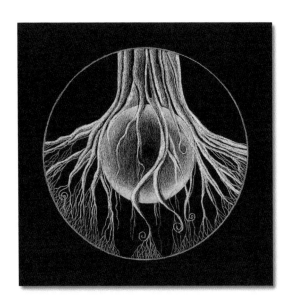

5. Roots - Under World - Throat

In this mandala you can see the roots of the Tree of Life, the Tree of Knowledge, the World Tree, or your Family Tree. We move from Animal Archetypes to the Archetype of the Tree to represent the upper three chakras. These upper three chakras are our ethereal or divine chakras that connect us to belief. Every belief system has a tree as a central unifying force within its creation or soul story. It is time to tap into your roots and send what does not serve you into the earth to mulch. Receive the life giving energy of the earth to strengthen you as you find your truth. Once you feel strong in your truth speak it with peace, compassion and love. As you speak your truth you are creating a new reality. This is your gift to the world. Located in your throat this chakra serves as the gateway for your inner and outer truth. Your throats carry the stories of your ancestors as they were shared through the spoken word before time began. You are being asked to speak your truth from a place of inner wisdom.

Before you speak it is important to heal the stories that you have buried and those that have uprooted you. You are being asked to find the deeper meaning that may have been hidden from you or misinterpreted through generations of story telling. These stories form the roots of your subconscious mind, also referred to as the unconscious self. Many stories were buried due to fear of being seen or heard. Others speak to your souls disconnection with the earth based on centuries of being uprooted from the land you came from. In both cases it is important to reclaim and heal these stories of your roots. You are still holding these stories in your subconscious mind. Now is the time to awaken your roots and heal your story. In many cultures the tree is seen as a way of traveling between worlds. The roots of the tree represent the lower world and have long been associated with death and the after life. It is the place where our earthly body rests. Early cultures lived in harmony with the lower world as they saw it as a place of dark beauty and replenishment. As our human body releases from our soul body it goes back to the lower world to be mulched by the earth. This is a natural process that provides nutrients to feed the roots of future generations. Mankind's fascination with death created stories about Gods and Goddesses that ruled the underworld. This obsession with the afterlife has formed the foundation for most of our modern day belief systems. Many involved a process of judgment that dates back thousands of years. Even the word Hell is a borrowed concept of an early Goddess in Germanic and Norse mythology. It is the energy of these stories that have been passed on through generations that continue to carry the belief of what the underworld is. When we look objectively at the entire tree we see that the roots look very similar to the branches. The concept of as above, so below should inspire you to claim your roots, heal your story and speak with truth. Your words will reach far and wide.

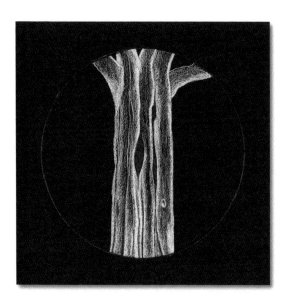

6. Trunk - Middle World - Third Eye

The Trunk of the tree represents your third eye chakra, your awakened conscious state or what Shamans call the middle world. It is a reminder to stand strong and stay present as you connect with your inner knowing and intuition. Trust what you are feeling and anchor it within your heart. Your heart will help you at the level of the soul to sort out what feels right. It may take practice and patience but now is the time for you to exercise this gift and not hide it from yourself or the world. As you practice opening your third eye and staying present in the moment you reclaim your inner wisdom. It may feel like imagination to you but there is a reason you are imagining it now. You are beginning to ask deeper questions within yourself that require you to trust. The third eye is located in the middle of your forehead and helps you see what is unseen. By awakening your intuitive eye you can see the tree trunk as a reflection of your true nature. Trees have inspired the mind and stirred the imagination of mankind.

Originally seen as ancestor spirits and helpers, they are also referred to as "The Standing People." Trees paved the way for humans to live on this earth by purifying the air we breathe. They inhale toxic carbon dioxide and exhale oxygen. They provide shelter, tools, food, medicine, fire and a spiritual connection to something beyond man himself. Man created communities within sacred groves of trees and sat in circle around fire provided by them. The inner rings of a tree are the record keepers of its life here on earth. This innermost core is the "heartwood" or essence of the tree. This core also represents your heart, reminding you that the core of who you are resides in your soul. Ancient Germanic Celts created an entire alphabet from trees. They saw trees as families and named then as such. The Oak family included oak, beech and chestnut. They were called Duir, which meant door. Someone who knew how to open the Duir or Door of an Oak was considered "Oakwise". These people became known as Druids, and were the visionary shamans of their tribe. Many early cultures from Siberia to the Americas believed in trees as a way to travel between worlds and gain insights and information. In essence they were traveling within them selves. They would gather information in the present moment from the middle world, lower world or upper world. The third eye of man shut down thousands of years ago as the doorways between worlds were closed due to fear and persecution. The great insights of life became the great mystery teachings as the known became unknown. In this very moment, you are being asked to awaken and make the unknown known. By being fully awake you can open your intuitive third eye and connect with your heart at the level of the soul. Stand strong and tall and be present in what is happening to you now. Reclaim your inner wisdom and see all that is out there for you. See that your life is filled with gifts and insights that will help you move forward.

7. Branches - Upper World - Crown

Our crown chakra represents our ability to reach out to the future just as branches reach up to the sky. The Upper World is considered our future world, super conscious, collective unconscious and collective consciousness. By connecting to the branches in the upper world we can begin to sense infinity and the knowing that we are not alone. We often access this world during dreamtime, meditation or prayer. You are being asked to go outside and connect with the sun, the moon and the stars above you. Do this during the day and the night. Become more aware of the cycles of the moon and the sun and the stars. Connect with the light that shines from each of them and notice how each makes you feel. Bring this light into your soul and remember that an entire universe sees you and is feeding you with life giving light and nourishing darkness. Stretch out your arms as you enjoy feeling all that is there for you. Our crown invites us to connect with other realms of reality.

The four heavenly realms of the Earth, Moon, Sun and Stars work in harmony with the four earthly winds of South, West, North and East thus creating an infinite cycle of birth, life, death, and rebirth. These great cycles inspired early cultures to celebrate the sunrise each morning, and the sunset each evening. The moon was honored in all its phases as it brought light to the night sky. They noticed how the lunar year of thirteen moons complimented the solar year and how nine moons was the approximate time it took for a baby to form in the belly of its mother. They also saw that the lunar years balanced each other as one year would have 13 new moons and the next year would have 13 full moons. From earth the sun and moon looked equal in size, creating the eyes of the universe among the stars. The lunar eye is the feminine eye, reflecting back both light and dark, knowing and mystery. The Greek word for moon is mense. The masculine solar eye creates a yearlong cycle of seasons, it sleeps at night so life can regenerate and prepare for the day ahead. Together they create balance and harmony for life on earth. The stars are representative of your cosmic third eye, revealing the bigger picture and greater cycles of the universe. The universe is reminding you that you originated from somewhere beyond this earth. Life began when space particles impacted oure earth billions of years ago. These particles all had a source. Together they created life. What you see today is an infinite variety of life forms that have adapted to a vast range of complex environments. These life forms come in all shapes, sizes and colors. Some are seen and some are not. It is in this unseen or unknown reality that the infinite Tree of Life resides. It is what you feel deep within your soul that tugs at you and reminds you that you are more than what you see here on earth. Stand tall and remember the knowledge that resides within. Stay grounded as you sink your roots deeper within the earth. Reach out and feel infinity.

Symbolic
Sacred Geometry

The word sacred has become synonymous with the concept of "Divine". The word "Geometry" comes from the Greek words Geos meaning, "Earth" and Metron meaning, "to measure". Together this translates as the "Divine Measuring of the Earth" or "Divine Earthly Measurements". In either case sacred geometry is mans way of understanding the relationship between nature and the cosmos by combining art and science to create divine order. According to Joseph Campbell in his book The Way of the Power Animals; "When mankind began measuring the movements of the planets and the stars, this led to the realization that the cosmos was mathematically ordered. This shifted the focus from animal and plant messengers to the night sky and the ever dying and self-resurrecting moon and the sun." Since both the moon and the sun were circular in shape and followed a circular path around earth it was easy to see the great circles of cosmic order. This desire for order and connection between the cosmos and man led to profound insights as well as the formation of religions and belief systems throughout the world. Leonardo Da Vinci (1452 – 1519), studied sacred geometry as a way to bridge art, science and divine order to create a more holistic view of our world. Today we are beginning to rediscover sacred geometry as a way to understand the divine nature of living in this world.

*"The square symbolizes the solid physical world
and the circle the spiritual and eternal.
Man bridges the gap between these two worlds."
- Leonardo Da Vinci -*

31

8. Circle - Root

The circle is a two-dimensional cross section of a sphere. It resides in your root chakra as the archetype of wholeness. Early man saw it as the symbol of divine creation, perfection and oneness. It represents both the manifest and the unmanifest. It cannot be contained nor defined. The essence of the circle exists in a dimension that transcends the linear world that it contains. It is unlimited in its potential. The circle has 360 equidistant points of light that surround the center point. Our present day solar calendar of 365 days is based on the 360 degrees of a circle. Because earth travels on an elliptical path five days were added to create continuity. The center point within the circle represents the seed of your soul and your desire to feel whole. Now is the time to plant a new intention for your soul. Whatever has been holding you is now releasing. Allow your roots to grow and believe in the unlimited potential of who you are. Trust that you can begin to manifest your new intention in all areas of your life.

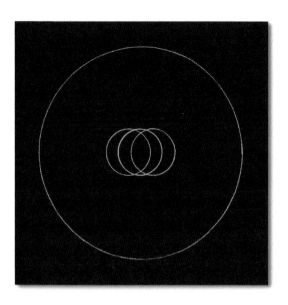

9. Vesica Piscis - Sacral

The Vesica Piscis is formed by the intersection of two circles whose centerpoints exactly touch. This symbolic intersection represents common ground, shared vision or mutual understanding between equal individuals. The shape of the human eye is a vesica piscis, and is seen as a mirror to the soul. The vesica piscis is also seen as a birth portal and resides in your sacral chakra. It symbolizes the creation of life itself. Here the one (individual) becomes two (mother, father), which creates another one (child). It is the ultimate symbol of the never-ending cycle of life. The central circle contains the shared essence of your soul. This is the chakra that holds your creative essence.   Look for a potential partnership or community that can support and inspire you to push through any fear or doubt.   Expand your concept of creation for everyone is an artist.   Enjoy being creative and remember there are no mistakes only insights. It is time for you to create and step outside your normal boundaries.

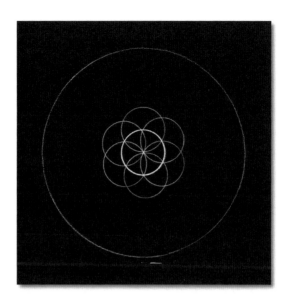

10. Seed of Life - Solar Plexus

The Seed of Life is made up of six circles that have divided from the one. Imagine the vesica piscis creating itself six times over in a rotation around the central circle. The central circle represents your soul and is the center point of your intention. The Seed of Life is often called the Genesis Pattern, as it reflects the six days of creation and the seventh day of rest. It also reveals the seven chakras or rays of your energy body. The seed of life resides within your solar plexus chakra reminding you of the power you hold. Your internal Sun quietly warms and incubates your intentions while the external Sun shines brightly upon you. Together they nourish you by providing you with life affirming energy. Fuel your inner confidence as you move forward in all aspects of your life. Connect with the power of the Sun to rejuvenate your core. Be open to the power that is growing within you, and how to use it wisely and peacefully. The light is shining within you and upon you. Step into it and enjoy.

11. Flower of Life - Heart

Adding 12 additional circles to the 7 circles of the Seed of Life creates the Flower of Life. This reveals an interlocking matrix of 19 circles. These 12 additional circles represent the twelve aspects of the zodiac and the twelve months of the year. The Zodiac "ring of animals" are epic stories held within the stars. The 7 independent circles represent the seven days of creation and the seven days of the week. When you focus on the six circles rotating around the central circle you can see that there are twelve separate infinity symbols. This is symbolic of the union of your inner and outer journey. The Flower of Life represents your soul as you remember that you are of the stars and of the earth. Each breath you take connects you to this fact. You are being asked to express a dream you planted almost a year ago. Now is the time to allow that dream to blossom. Gather flowers you love as you connect to your souls true intention. Express your new reality and allow your soul to reveal itself.

12. Fruit of Life - Throat

Adding 42 additional circles to the 19 circles within the Flower of Life creates the Fruit of Life. This reveals an interlocking matrix of 61 circles. The outer row of 24 circles represents the 24 hours in a day, while the 60 circles rotating around the central circle are the 60 minutes within one hour or 60 seconds within one minute. The thirteeen independent circles represent a lunar year that consists of 13 moon cycles. The lunar year alternates between 13 full moons (yang/male) and 13 new moons (yin/female). The Fruit of Life reveals the wisdom of the internal and external aspects of your life. It holds the great mystery and organization of your world. Mense is the Greek word for Moon. The word Men is a word that is both male and female. New opportunities are manifesting in your life now. Meditate on what this may be for one full moon cycle (approx 29 days) beginning today. Express your thoughts on paper until the cycle is complete. Insights will be revealed that will help you make this a reality.

13. Knowledge of Life - Third Eye

The Knowledge of Life is revealed by connecting the center of each of the 13 "feminine" circles of the Fruit of Life with 78 "masculine" lines. This matrix is called Metatron's Cube. It appears when the circular/receptive world of your right-brain is connected with the linear/logical world of your left-brain. In Jewish mysticism Metatron is the Archangel who holds the secrets for mans return to the Garden of Eden where both the Tree of Life and the Tree of Knowledge reside. By meditating on the image of Metatron's Cube you will notice that it is both two-dimensional and three-dimensional. Its simplicity and complexity can provide profound insights into the infinite nature of your universe and your self. In Hebrew Metatron "metered" is the male aspect of God while Shekinah "dwelling" is the female aspect of God.   It is time for you to trust both your rational and intuitive mind. New knowledge is forming in your consciousness. You can now begin to see how everything is interrelated and interdependent.

14. Star of Life - Crown

The Star of life is revealed within the wisdom of the Knowledge of Life. This symbol is also called the Merkaba, an ancient Hebrew word for Chayot or Chariot. It is seen as Gods throne or chariot that carries mans soul to heaven. The Star of Life or Merkaba reminds us that our soul comes from the stars and will return to the stars. The Merkaba (mer = light, ka = spirit, and ba = body) represents the joining together of our earthly soul with our divine soul to create our soul body. The downward triangle holds our three lower chakras, the upward facing triangle holds our three upper chakras. They merge together at the midpoint of our soul body within the heart chakra, the place of our infinite soul. From this place we can begin to understand how our soul travels through time and space. The star of life is reminding you to honor the stars that shine upon you and to connect with them. This is a good time to see which stars or star systems speak to your soul. Ask your soul to journey to them during dreamtime for insights.

Mythic
Elements of Nature

The concept of elemental solids has been known before antiquity. Ancient Neolithic cultures carved images of them onto stone balls over a thousand years before they became known as the Platonic Solids. Ancient Greek philosophers and mathematicians studied the idea of basic geometric shapes as the building blocks of life and the universe. Some credit Pythagoras (570 BCE – 495 BCE) and Theaetetus (417 BCE – 369 BCE) with their discovery. Plato (424 BCE – 347 BCE), a student of Socrates, wrote of them extensively in his dialogue Timaeus, as the building blocks of life represented by the four elements of earth, water, fire and air. Aristotle identified a fifth element he called Aether, but did not see it as a solid. Euclid (323 BCE – 283 BCE) brought them together and named them the Platonic Solids and gave precise mathematical descriptions in his book Elements. This vast body of knowledge went virtually underground until Johannes Kepler (1571 – 1630) a German astronomer added the sphere as a sixth solid. He saw the sphere as a container for each of the five platonic solids. He also tried to connect the solids with the six known planets of Mercury, Venus, Earth, Mars, Jupiter and Saturn. In Euclidean geometry a Platonic solid is seen as a regular, convex polyhedron. The faces are congruent, regular polygons, with the same number of faces meeting at each vertex. Their symmetry continues to provide inspiration for art, science and the elegance of our universe.

"Geometry will draw the soul toward truth
and create the spirit of philosophy"
- Plato -

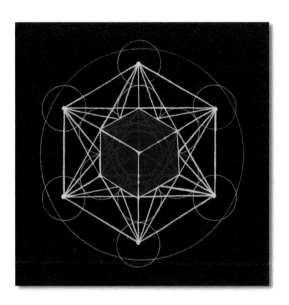

15. Earth - Hexahedron - Root

The Hexahedron or "cube" has six equal square faces. It represents solidarity, strength, order and foundation. It is symbolic of Earth and is energetically equivalent to our muscular skeletal body. Our root chakra connects us with earth and to our physical body. The saying "we are what we eat" is completely true! It is the earth that makes all food possible. Earth is often seen as the Archetypal Mother, nurturing and receptive yet strong and resourceful. As ancient asteroids and other space particles collided with Earth, they impregnated her with seeds. These seeds carried elements necessary to create life. It is from these seeds that all life on earth was born. This understanding will help you to deepen your relationship with the mothering intelligence of Earth. Allow yourself to feel intimately connected within her and her within you. Practice gratitude for all that she gives to you. Live from this place of gratitude as you eat, breathe, sleep and walk through your everyday life here on earth.

16. Water - Icosahedron - Sacral

The Icosahedron has twenty equal triangular faces. The Icosahedron is symbolic of water. It is the dual or partner of the Dodecahedron, the element of Ether. When paired together they represent the structure of Carbon. You are considered a Carbon being and water acts as a transport system within your body, providing your cells with neccesary nutrients for life. Your body consists of roughly 75% water. Our earth is also over 70% water. Water is symbolic of the creative force of nature. It is both replenishing and destructive, which can create a sense of duality or inner conflict. These opposing forces give you the ability to create or to destroy. This is the essence of Chaos, which in turn leads to order and the creation of something new. Water helps you see that the power of Chaos is a creative force that ultimately brings balance to your life in a new way. Connect with the power of water as you cleanse and replenish. Flow with the changes that are flowing within you.

17. Fire - Tetrahedron - Solar Plexus

The Tetrahedron has four equal triangular faces. The Tetrahedron is symbolic of Fire. Fire releases heat and light through a process known as combustion. It is found in the sun and the stars and felt within our digestive system. Just like water, the power of fire can be both beneficial and destructive. Your body is like a finely tuned engine, or furnace, that maintains a steady temperature of 98.6° Fahrenheit. This is known as homeostasis, a natural process that your body performs to adapt to change and maintain equilibrium. It is important to find the right balance or temperature when working with fire in all aspects of your life. Eating a healthy diet as well as generating healthy thoughts and behaviors is critical in maintaining equilibrium. Fire is a powerful force for releasing and cleansing your emotional and energetic body. It has been the central focus in sustaining life on earth and in sacred ceremony since the dawn of man. Meditate with fire as you balance the power growing within.

18. Love - Star Tetrahedron - Heart

The Star Tetrahedron is not one of the original Platonic Solids, yet it holds a very distinct place within geometric order. Also called a double tetrahedron or Merkaba it is created by the joining of an upward-pointing tetrahedron, representing male, fire and blade with a downward-facing tetrahedron, representing female, water and chalice. Together they are interlocked and interpenetrating representing the power of love. The Greek philosopher Empedocles (490 BCE – 430 BCE) is credited with officially identifying the four ultimate forces as: fire, air, water and earth. He saw that these forces of nature were eternally brought into union and parted from each other through love and strife. Love is the power that attracts different forms of matter while strife separates them. Empedocles saw this ultimate relationship between love and strife as the essence of our soul. Love and strife are both influencing your life right now. Allow your life to shift in a direction that feels loved.

19. Air - Octahedron - Throat

The Octahedron has eight equal triangular faces. It is made up of two four-sided triangles of equal proportion that meet at the base. The Octahedron is symbolic of air. The upward and downward facing triangles represent cosmic balance. Air is considered both hot/dry and cold/wet. Greek philsophers saw two levels of air. "Aer" is the dimmer atmosphere that we breathe which surrounds our earth. "Aether" is the brighter air above the clouds associated with the divine. In Hindu tradition air is called Vayu, which is related to Prana. Prana is the act of breathing in life. Unlike Greek philosophy, air is not one of the five classical elements in Chinese philosophy: (wood, fire, earth, metal and water). For them air is seen as Chi or life force energy. Literally translated as breath. Air is the creative essence of life; breath creates life through vibrations that ripple throughout time and space. You are being asked to become more aware of the air around you and the air you breathe. Bring more balance into your life.

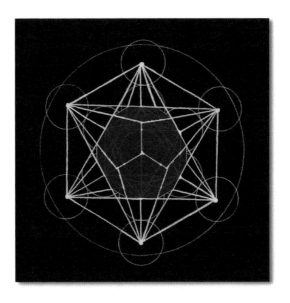

20. Ether - Dodecahedron - Third Eye

The Dodecahedron has 12 equal pentagonal faces. The Dodecahedron is symbolic of Ether, which is unknown and unseen. Plato saw it as a model for the twelvefold division of the Zodiac. Aristotle felt it was the element of the heavens also called Aether or Ether that represents "divine thought" or will and is the archetype of life. In 2003 cosmologists suggested that our universe consisted of 12 curved pentagons joined together in a sphere, which could be 30 billion light years across. Today CERN's Large Hadron Collider, in Switzerland, is discovering that 96% of our universe is made up of "dark matter and dark energy". Both of which remain unseen and unknown. The Higgs boson, nicknamed the "God Particle" could explain how mass is created by bringing energy and matter together. The mysterious nature of our universe is a gift that encourages you to seek answers. Embrace this gift as you expand your mind to all possibilities. Begin to see that nothing is impossible for you.

21. Light - Sphere - Crown

The Sphere is symbolic of our universe. Plato and Kepler both felt that each of the Platonic solids fit within a sphere. Spheres within spheres can be seen as multi-verses or multiple universes. The sphere is also symbolic of your soul for it contains all that you are. Visible light is only seen within the spectrum of light produced by spheres such as the Sun, Stars and Moon. Black light is considered ultra-violet light, which means "uber (above) violet" which is invisible to the human eye. What we see in a black lightbulb is the violet glow created by phosphor, a substance that emits visible light in response to radiation, which is also light. UVA & UVB are two types of ultra-violet light that are generated by the Sun but are invisible to our eyes. Astrophysicists now see that 96% of our universe contains invisible light or dark energy. Connect with color and appreciate the mystery of invisible light. Bring color into your life in a new way to help you shed light on a situation that has been puzzling you.

Energetic
Chakras of our Soul Body

Our physical body is the body we see and feel everyday. It is the body we love and nurture to live a strong and healthy life. Through our physical body we are able to delight in the senses and experience the amazing gift of feeling alive and what it means to be human. At the same time we have a more subtle body that resides within and surrounds our physical body called the energy body or soul body. For the most part it is invisible to the human eye as it is pure energy. This energy body shares the same anatomical structure that mirrors our physical body. Our physical body is made up of skin, bones, muscles, organs, blood and other tissues. Our energy body is organized into seven primary chakras or spinning wheels of energy. Our chakras connect our energy body with our physical body, which is why we often manifest physical symptoms from an emotional experience. This can range from feeling your heart expand with love to feeling punched in the stomach by harsh words. All of these emotions are carried within our energy body. When we hold wounded emotions and don't release them we can begin to manifest physical symptoms. It is important to listen and heal our emotional body just as it is to heal our physical body. The following pages will provide insights for each chakra for healing your energy body through the use of food, plants, crystals, essential oils, movement and intentions.

"We are not human beings having a spiritual experience.
We are spiritual beings having a human experience."
- Teilhard de Chardin

"Awakening to one's true Self-radiant nature is ultimate spiritual and emotional healing."
- Rajita Sivananda (Dr. Judith Cornell)

22. Root Chakra

Listen to your root chakra and sense what it is asking of you. Spend time outside connecting to nature. It is important for you to feel grounded and to trust that the earth will give you what you need. Release what no longer serves you and make healthier choices to create a strong foundation. The root chakra is located at the base of your spine. This mandala contains a four-sided square representing the four directions of East, South, West and North. Within the square is a downward V holding an awakening spiral. The V symbolizes the archetypal feminine energy of the womb of Mother Earth. The awakening spiral represents the Serpent of Light or Kundalini energy that rests at the base of our root chakra. When we trust the process of releasing negative emotions from our energy body to the earth we receive nourishment from the earth in return. This creates a healthy and loving relationship within our root chakra that brings us into harmony with the earth.

As we live in harmony with the earth we trust the mothering love she provides. This supports the healing journey to our awakened soul.

Basic information about the Root Chakra

Goals: To release, feel rooted & nourished by mother earth.
Practice: non-judgment, non-attachment, beauty and grace.
Malfunction: Inability to trust or feel grounded. Leads to issues surrounding the process of elimination both physically and energetically as well as fear and or general anxiety
Symptoms: Obesity, hemorrhoids, constipation, sciatica, and muscular- skeletal disorders. Night terrors and panic attacks.
Plant Ally: Sage for cleansing and grounding.
Essential Oils: Ginger, Sandalwood, Juniper, Clove.
Foods: Root vegetables, ginger, turmeric, clove and protien.
Stones and Crystals: Iron, Basalt, Granite, Petrified Wood, Ruby, Garnet, Bloodstone, Red Jasper, Smoky Quartz, Obsidian, Black Tourmaline, Hematite, Snowflake Obsidian.

Root Movement: Getting Grounded - Close your eyes and rest your hands at your side. Feel the earth supporting you and your feet grounding down. Scan your body for tenseness and release it through your root chakra to the earth. Feel the subtle movement of your body with each breath, expanding and contracting. With your eyes closed soften yourself until you feel a shift as your body finds its natural place on earth. From this place imagine sending roots from your hands and feet deep into the earth. Feel the layers of stone, sand and water as your roots explore and grow. Stay in this place long enough to feel connected and then bring that energy into your body as nourishment. Send gratitude to the earth for supporting you and loving you unconditionally. Open your eyes and shake your arms and legs to release.

23. Sacral Chakra

Listen to your sacral chakra and be aware of the choices you are making and the lifestyle you are creating. Release any fears or judgment that may be holding you. Start a new routine that pleases your senses. Relax your body and allow yourself to flow and feel passionate about life. The sacral chakra is located within the area of your reproductive system. It encourages the ongoing flow of creative energy. When we place judgment on our self or others we restrict the flow of creative expression. This flow is vital to life. As the harmony of opposites flows throughout our every day lives, we are able to reveal and receive information that helps us feel balanced and whole. By understanding this dynamic we can step out of fear and judgment and into peace. This is the essence of what it means to be human as we are continually creating something new. Creativity is not limited to art, music and literature. It is expressed through the choices, words and actions we make in everyday life.

Each moment of your life is unique and presents opportunities for the flow of creative expression.

Basic information about the Sacral Chakra

Goals: Fluidity, pleasure, relaxation, fearlessness, peace

Practice: Fearlessness, certainty, non-engagement.

Malfunction: Fear and judgment create a sense of duality and isolation. Fear of change prohibits the creative process and shuts down the flow of life force energy.

Symptoms: Stiffness, sexual problems, isolation, emotional instability or numbness. PTSD (Post Traumatic Stress Disorder) stimulates the flight, fight or freeze syndrome.

Plant: Jasmine for sensuality.

Essential Oils: Jasmine, Neroli, Orange Blossom, Ylang Ylang, Cypress, Patchouli and Myrtle

Foods: Liquids - fruit and vegetable juices, herbals teas to add fluids and replenish the body.

Stones and Crystals: Coral, Carnelian, Orange Amber, Orange/Dark Citrine, Peach Aventurine, Orange Calcite.

Sacral Movement: Going with the Flow - Stand with your feet slightly apart. Place hands on each hip and begin to sway your hips side to side. Drop your arms and allow them to move any way they want. Widen your movements and incorporate more flow. Rotate your hips in rhythmic circles moving your pelvis gently forward and back. It may feel silly or strange at first, but just let go and loosen up. Imagine you are in the water and it is flowing all around you and through you. This is sort of like being a belly dancer. They are comfortable expressing their sensuality through the movement of their body. Continue this movement until you are smiling from the inside and feel relaxed on the outside. Release all judgment and worry and allow yourself to go with the flow.

24. Solar Plexus Chakra

Listen to your solar plexus and sense what it is asking of you. Fuel yourself by finding the courage to bring forth what is within you. Eat healthy foods and drink plenty of water to maintain a balanced diet. It is also important to feed yourself with healthy intentions. Feel the warmth in your belly and know it is your internal sun providing you with strength and courage. The solar plexus chakra is located in the stomach area of our physical body and is connected to our digestive, lymphatic and immune system. It is symbolic of the fire that burns within us. Our body behaves like a finely tuned engine, or furnace, that maintains a body temperature of 98.6° Fahrenheit. It performs what is known as homeostasis, the bodies natural ability to change and balance as needed to maintain equilibrium of temperature. The fire in our bellies reminds us to balance our tempers as we continue to grow and gain confidence in ourselves. This is necessary for us to feel both peaceful and powerful at the same time.

We do this by feeding ourselves a balanced diet of healthy foods and positive intention. With every action we create a reaction.

Basic information about the Solar Plexus Chakra
Goals: Vitality, confidence, will, joy and sweetness
Practice: Integrity, becoming mindful of your actions and thoughts, transparency, stop hiding from yourself. Transform your negative thoughts into positive journey statements.
Malfunction: Lack of confidence leads to a sense of timidity and allows other to dominate your life. Feeling unempowered
Symptoms: Ulcers, acid reflux, indigestion, fatigue, withdrawal, depression, apathy, liver dysfunction
Plant: Sunflower for nourishment.
Essential Oils: Lemon, Grapefruit, Juniper, Lavender, Fennel, Sandalwood, Cardamom, Champa Flower
Foods: Complex carbohydrates – legumes, potatoes, whole grain breads, pastas and cereals for energy and strength
Stones & Crystals: Tiger Eye, Yellow Amber, Citrine, Gold, Gold Calcite, Topaz, Yellow Jade. Gold Quartz, Pyrite

Solar Plexus Movement: Stoking the Fire - Sit on the ground or on a stool. Clasp your hands together behind the base of your spine. Breathe in four deep breaths through your nose and hold. Then begin breathing in and out through your nose with shallow breaths that stoke the fire in your belly 7 times in and 7 times out. After that take one deep breath in and out and relax. Repeat this same sequence with your hands clasped above your head. Relax. Bring your hands to your Solar Plexus and repeat sequence for third time. Scan your chakra to feel the fire in your belly, imagine it as a ball that you can hold with your hands. Feel what size it is or how warm or cool it is. When you are ready place this ball of life force energy into your solar plexus as energetic nourishment.

25. Heart Chakra

Listen to your heart chakra and feel your heart open and close based on events, emotions or energy around you. Become aware of what helps your heart to open and what causes it to close. Both are necessary just like sleeping at night and being awake during the day. Think of your heart as a Rose that is filled with beauty. Use Rose oil, Roses or Rose Quartz to help you protect your heart as you enter this process of healing and trusting in the power of unconditional love. Located in the area of our heart and lungs the heart chakra represents the mid point for our energy body. The lower three chakras and the upper three chakras are anchored in the heart which is also the place of the soul. The two triangles represent the lower chakras and upper chakras. When they intersect they form a Merkaba (spirit, light, body). The heart chakra is the place of our true intentions. It is the core of who we are and anchors us to the core of the earth and to the core of our source.

The heart releases 60% more electromagnetic energy than our brains. It is our power center, and its fuel is unconditional love. The Heart Math institute is showing how our heart informs our brain versus our brain informing our heart. This awareness opens up a new world of sharing love within your self and also with others. Be love...

Basic information about the Heart Chakra
Goals: Balance, compassion, unconditional love
Practice: Stop hiding from yourself, love unconditionally.
Malfunction: A closed heart does not unconditionally love itself or others. The opposite of love is fear and when we feel fear our heart becomes hard, angry or shut down
Symptoms: Loneliness, codependence, resentment, jealousy
Plant: Rose for love...
Essential Oils: Rose, Carnation, and Lily of the Valley
Foods: Vegetables greens, broccoli, cucumbers, asparagus
Stones & Crystals: Rose Quartz, Peridot, Emerald, Green and Pink Tourmaline, Green Jade, Green Aventurine, Green Fluorite, Malachite, Kunzite, Copper, Serpentine, Pink Opal, Green Quartz , Pink and Green sea glass.

Heart Chakra Movement: Opening to Love - Stand in a comfortable position and bring your hands to your heart in a prayer pose. Gently release your hands towards the earth and open the circle as wide as possible extending your arms to your side and bring in all the love from nature back into your heart. Once palms are back in prayer pose reach for the sky and circle as wide as possible extending your arms to bring in all the love from the universe back into your heart. Repeat both movements coming back to your heart in prayer pose. Gently repeat eight times in a continual figure eight pattern. Feel your heart expand and imagine loving all of you and what is around you.

26. Throat Chakra

Listen to your throat chakra and sense if you are being asked to speak up more or less? Are you speaking truthfully, or do you not know your truth? Either way, the throat chakra will help you open and heal so you can speak your truth from a place of love, compassion and peaceful power. Located in our throats the throat chakra serves as the gateway for our inner and outer truth. The interlocking triangles represent the union of above and below. This is symbolic of speaking from a place of both love and wisdom. Our words also create the world we live in. For this reason it is important to clear yourself of fears and untruths, so you can speak your truth yet also practice peace. The words you speak are the fruits of your wisdom. They are the gifts you choose to share with the world. That is why it is so important to use your words wisely. Every word carries a vibration that ripples throughout the universe. Sound carries long distances and impacts places and people we do not see.

These vibrations are the essence of creation throughout the universe. From this place of awareness we realize how our words truly do create our reality.

Basic information about the Throat Chakra

Goals: Clear communication, creativity, resonance and truth

Practice: Be true to your word, and see how your words or your silence affects you and the world around you.

Malfunction: Losing your voice due to untruths or fear of speaking the truth. Not knowing how to speak with compassion

Symptoms: Shyness, silence, lying, sore throats, stiff neck.

Throat Chakra Plant: Gardenia for inspiration

Essential Oils: Blue Chamomile, Gardenia, Ylang Ylang, Bergamont, Spruce, Davana

Foods: Fruits, especially juicy fruits such as oranges, lemons, limes, apples, pears, cherries, mangos, kiwi, peaches, melons

Stones & Crystals: Amazonite, Celestite, Sodalite, Angelite, Aquamarine, Blue Calcite, Turquoise, Azurite, Chrysocolla, Blue Fluorite, Blue Lace Agate, Blue Kyanite, Lapis, Sodalite

Throat Chakra Movement: Singing with Love - Sing or chant by repeating the Mantra of the throat 22 times:

"Om Padme Ham Namah"
(Open the Lotus of my Throat with love).

27. Third Eye Chakra

Listen to your third eye chakra and let go of the monkey mind that is causing you to feel scattered or stuck. Your third eye is located in the middle of your forehead. It connects the frontal lobe of our brain with the limbic system (Amygdala, Pineal Gland, etc). This information is then anchored within our heart. Slow down and breathe, quiet your mind and connect with your heart. From this place you will begin to see what is truly within you. This will help you receive information from your heart where you can send it back to both sides of your brain and see the whole picture. Basic Intelligence is one aspect of being human, emotional intelligence is another aspect. Both are important, but we have placed far more energy towards improving our basic intelligence. Now is the time to improve your emotional intelligence by connecting your heart with your thoughts. Opening your third eye allows you to see with your heart instead of your eyes. This will help you to see what your soul truly wants you to see.

The more we trust our inner knowing the more our third eye will open. The (IQ) intelligence quotient and (EQ) emotional quotient can become one. From this place of awareness we reconnect with both aspects of our self and begin to feel whole. The divine is within us and the knowledge is within us, our third eye is the singular eye that sees the oneness of everything. Science sees this as the pre-frontal neo-cortex, it is only found in mammals. It allows us to sense our world from a literal perspective. Our limbic system interprets it and sends it to our heart that provides an emotional response. This is known as intuition.

Basic information about the Third Eye Chakra
Goals: Trust your intuition and inner knowing
Practice: Dream your world into being. Trust in your knowing.
Malfunction: Not trusting your intuition and or inner knowing. Closing your mind to new ideas or ways of thinking
Symptoms: Headaches, nightmares, feeling stuck in your head
Plant: Fruit and Nut Blossoms
Essential Oils: Peppermint, Rosemary, and Lavender
Foods: Feasts for the Eyes! Colorful and Healthy
Stones & Crystals: Iolite, Amethyst, Sugilite, Charoite, Purple Fluorite, Tanzanite

Third Eye Movement: Letting go of the Ego - Bring hands to prayer pose at center of forehead and become aware of the monkey mind or ego. Breathe gently and relax. Let go of thought and open your heart through your third eye let thoughts and feelings flow through you.

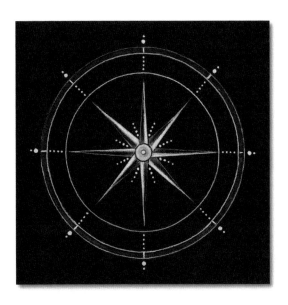

28. Crown Chakra

Listen to your higher self and sense what it is asking of you. Connect with the stars as you stand on earth and feel what your soul is yearning for. Open your mind and your heart to all that is out there and see what feels right for you. You are not alone and only you can define the undefined for yourself. Imagine opening your crown chakra like a lotus flower to help you heal or deepen your connection to source until you realize that you are an infinite soul that will never be alone. The crown chakra is located at the top of your head and represents our belief system and connection to the universe. Carl Jung believed that the human psyche was "by nature religious" and that the mystical heart was at the core of all belief. Through our crown chakra we connect with the mystical aspect of who we are and where we see ourselves in the universe. There are over a 1000 names for God, yet it is also nameless and formless. It is seen as the Great Mystery and both the Cosmic Void and the Cosmic Consciousness.

We each have the unique ability to connect with our own sense of how we live in this vast universe. Remain open to all possibilities without judgment. Stars have long held great mystery to us as they fill the night sky. It is through direct revelation and a feeling of interconnectedness that early man saw the stars as their ancestors. When you go out at night notice the beauty of the dark night and see which star is calling you. Stars point in all directions, discover your path...

Basic information about the Crown Chakra

Goals: Experience a spiritual connection so you are not alone.

Practice: Allow your mind to step out of the way of your soul.

Malfunction: Feeling alone in the universe, disconnected from your source and your soul. Thinking there is no purpose

Symptoms: Confusion, apathy, loss of purpose, deep sense of isolation, sadness and despair. Believing that this is all there is and feeling that death marks the end of everything.

Plant: Lotus Flower

Essential Oils: Violet, Lavender, Neroli, and Frankincense

Foods: Clear water

Stones & Crystals: Clear Quartz Crystal, Herkimer Diamond, Selenite, Alexandrite, Diamonds, Apophyllite

Crown Movement: A River of Light - Stand in a comfortable position and use both hands representing the masculine and feminine forces of nature. Move your hands up and down your body as if weaving them together. Imagine the Serpent of Light flowing from the base of your spine up to your crown chakra and circling back to your root only to begin again. Now imagine the serpent of light entering your crown chakra and flowing to your root, circling back up again. Repeat 7 times.

Sacred
Beliefs of Mankind

Mankind's original spiritual practice began over 50,000 years ago and was passed on through storytelling and ceremony weaving a rich tapestry of cultural heritage and religious tradition. Nature originally inspired many of the beliefs that form the basis of today's world religions. The desire to know how a souls travel through lifetimes and how to connect the heavens with the earth in this life created epic stories. These stories soon incorporated the idea of Gods and Goddesses who ruled the heavens and the earth. Over time these stories created wounds for they became sources of conflict and separation within our selves and with each other. Bringing awareness to these stories helps us to see how they continue to inform our collective unconsciousness. From this place of awareness we can become more conscious and heal the wounds of separation and judgment. The wise shamans, seers and sages believe these ancient stories are written in our hearts. As we heal our hearts and open our minds we honor those who came before us and clear a new way of living for our children. When we reconnect with our true nature as being both human and divine we will see that our diversity is what makes us strong. When we see through that walls that divide us and begin to focus on our shared roots we will see in our hearts that we are all sharing the same dream of love and living in peace.

"The mystic discovers symbols. . .
symbols are windows through which we can view
the essential nature of our being."
- Ngakpa Chogyam -

*"All religions, arts and sciences
are branches of the same tree.
All these aspirations are directed
toward ennobling man's life,
lifting it from the sphere
of mere physical existence
and leading the individual towards freedom. "
- Albert Einstein -*

29. Indigenous - Root

Indigenous means original or aboriginal people. The circular cross is found in indigenous cultures throughout the world honoring the circular and linear aspects of life. Paganism is "to be from nature". Pagans created the Celtic cross as a solar calendar that reflected the seasons within the great cycle of life. The word Shaman comes from a Tungus speaking tribe in Siberia. It is closely related to Sramana a Sanskrit word for, the one who strives. Samadhi is another Sanskrit word for a state of higher consciousness. Those attaining Samadhi became known as Shramanas, forest yogis or traveling ones. Shamans created a bridge to help man evolve from a primal existence into human consciousness. The shaman journeyed into the upper world and the under world to meet with wise spirits. They journeyed into the middle world to meet with the souls of their people, and the spirits of the animals they hunted to create healing and harmony. Shamanism is interconnected with nature versus being in opposition to it.

Siberian and Mongolian shamans saw the universe as a living being with the pole star as the celestial nail. They decorated drums with the constellation of the Great Bear or the World Tree called Tuuru. Tuuru was considered a cosmic ladder that reached to the North Star in the upper world and down into Earth in the lower world. The Germanic Celts believed all trees had spirits and saw them as benevolent ancestors. Oak trees were named "Duir" or door. A person who was "Oakwise" became a Druid for they knew how to open the door of an Oak and travel between worlds. They created sacred poles made from trees and placed them in open areas as a way to connect the Earth and the Sky. These poles functioned as a compass during the daylight hours and an astronomical tool for tracking stars at night. In Norse tradition the World Tree is called Yggdrisil, or Odin's horse. Odin was a God who traveled through the nine worlds of the World Tree. The World Tree runs through the earth's core acting as a pole that the earth rotates around. The Celestial Tree is seen as a pole that runs through the center of the Milky Way galaxy. Connect with the trees in your life as a way to connect with your roots. Always remember that you are of the earth and of the stars. Now is the time to learn more about yourself and your ancestors. Uncover the stories of joy as well as heartache. Heal the wound stories by honoring the pain, recieving the insights and releasing what no longer serves you with forgiveness and love. Do this for yourself, your ancestors and the next seven generations to come.

"I was seeing in a sacred manner the shape of all things in the Spirit, and the Shape of all Shapes as they must live together like one being and I saw that the sacred hoop of my people was one of many hoops that made one circle, wide as daylight and as starlight, and in the center grew one mighty flowering tree to shelter all the children of one mother and one father. And I saw that it was holy."
- Black Elk -

30. Taoism - Sacral

Taoism believes that nature is in a continual balance between Yin and Yang, dark and light. Taoism helps us balance the sacred feminine and masculine within our sacral chakra. Taoism is based on indigenous beliefs that originated with the early Wu Shamans in China before 5000 BCE. These women were healers, rainmakers and dream interpreters who worked directly with plants, minerals, and animals, to journey deep into the earth, or high into the sky. Tao, or 'the way', embodies the harmony of opposites. Taoism believes that nature is continually balancing between Yin and Yang. In the Taoist creation myth, Wu-Ji is limitless and produces the delimited Tai-Ji that divides into heaven (Yang) and earth (Yin). Heaven and earth rejoin when man (Yang) and woman (Yin) mate thus experiencing supreme unity. Yin and Yang are often described in terms of sunlight moving over a mountain. Yin is the feminine shady place or North Slope where the shadow is cast by the sun shining on the mountain.

It is slow, soft, yielding, diffuse, cold, wet, tranquil; water, earth, moon and nighttime. Yang is the masculine sunny place or South Slope that is the brightly lit portion. It is fast, hard, solid, focused, hot, dry, or aggressive; fire, sky, sun and daytime. The dots within Yin and Yang symbolize that each contains aspects of the other. Taoists believe that since nature is a continual balance between Yin and Yang, that any shift to one extreme or the other will be self-defeating, and short-lived. Taoism shifted from a matriarchal society to a patriarchal one around 2500 BCE when they began focusing on morally perfected Sage-kings. King Wen created the Earthly Bagua in 1150 BCE as a tool for everyday living. The Bagua was thought to originate when Heaven and Earth mated giving birth to three daughters and three sons. This created a family of eight that correspond with the eight directions, the seasons of the year and the eight different forces of nature. (Earth, Lake, Sky, Water, Mountain, Thunder, Wind-Wood, Fire) It also incorporates the five Chinese elements of fire, metal, water, wood and earth. Lao Tzu (590 BCE) is seen as the offical father of Taoism and is credited with writing the Daodejing or "Book of the Way and its Power". Taoists practice Inner Alchemy to create spiritual union. They see that everything is both receptive feminine Yin energy, and expansive masculine Yang energy. Chi, or energy, exists in all aspects of life. The process of improving the flow of Chi throughout your life and your home became known as Feng Shui, which means Wind Water. Chi rides the wind and scatters energy, but is retained by water. Allow yourself to flow through the currents of your life. Do not fight what you perceive as "dark" for only when you look into the darkness will you find what the dark reveals.

"The softest things in the world
over comes the hardest things in the world."
- Lao Tzu -

31. Hinduism - Solar Plexus

Agni, God of Fire, is the first God mentioned in the Rigveda written around 1400 BCE. Hinduism sees Brahman as the Creator God who manifests as multiple Gods and Goddesses. Before the Vedas the Indus Valley culture believed in a matriarchal Trimurti. Devi was the Divine Heavenly Goddess, Tara was the Earth Mother Goddess and Maya was the Goddess of illusion and fate. Maya was depicted as a spider that wove a web of illusion that challenged man to see if life was real or not real. It was the responsibility of man to create their fate. The Banyan Tree is symbolic of the multiplicity of Hindu belief. It is seen as rooted in the heavens and bearing its fruit on earth. All the gods and goddesses, all the elements and cosmic principles are held in its branches. Every one is rooted in Brahman, who is seen as the trunk of the sacred tree. Devi is the divine from which the tree grows. Brahman, Vishnu and Shiva are now seen as the patriarchal Trimurti. These three aspects of God are paired with Goddesses.

Vishnu the preserver is paired with Lakshmi the Goddess of wealth and fortune. Shiva the destroyer God is paired with four goddesses: Parvarti, Kali, Durga and Shakti. Brahaman the Creator God is paired with Sarasvati the Goddess of wisdom, art and poetry.

Aum - symbol of Hinduism, the primordial sound of creation. Aum is a reflection of absolute reality, Adi without beginning & Anadi without end. It has three curves, one semicircle, and a dot. The lower curve is the waking conscious state. The upper curve is the unconscious state. The middle curve signifies the dream state, where consciousness turns inward. The dot signifies the fourth state of consciousness, which looks neither outwards nor inwards. This blissful state is the ultimate goal as it illuminates the other three. The semi-circle symbolizes Maya who creates the illusion of separation.

Dharma – the purpose you are born with. When a person's soul reincarnates into a new body their dharma is based on the state of mind at death as well as their desires and karma.

Karma – right action. Each soul creates its unique destiny according to karma, the universal law of action and reaction.

Samsara – wheel of life, a cycle of repeated life, death, rebirth and birth. Reincarnation is a basic belief in Hinduism.

Moksha – liberation from the cycle of Samsara. The goal of most Hindus is moksha (liberation) from this perpetual cycle. Hinduism has many paths called yoga to achieve this goal.

Bhakti – is a path or yoga that leads towards spiritual fulfillment. Bhakti is the original practice of pure devotion and selfless service to a personal God.

It is time for you to find your soul's unique purpose and path.

"You are what your deep, driving desire is.
As is your desire, so is your will.
As is your will, so is your deed.
As is your deed, so is your destiny."
– Upanishads

32. Buddhism - Heart

Buddha taught people to live from the heart. Siddhartha Gautama was born a Hindu Prince around 623 BCE. His father a Warrior King sheltered him from the world. One day Siddhartha left the palace and saw an old man, an ill man, a dead man, and a suffering man. He saw that suffering was the inevitable end of life. He came back to the palace and renounced himself as Prince and seeking to understand the meaning of suffering. After many years of questioning and meditation he decided to meditate in a cave and restrict the intake of food or water during their meditation. Siddhartha went into a deep state of meditation that he did not eat or drink at all. Eventually a young girl found Siddhartha who was close to death and convinced him to drink water. She began bringing food to him until he was strong enough to walk out of the cave. Frustrated with himself for almost dying and still not understanding the meaning of suffering, he saw how death would have stopped him from helping others.

At the age of 35 he sat under a large fig tree or Bodhi Tree to contemplate what had just happened. As he sat under the tree a large pod fell on his head. He instantly realized he had the choice to feel like a victim or to see it as a gift. He now understood how mankind could choose to be free of suffering. This transformed him into the "Buddha" or enlightened one. Buddha dedicated the next 46 years of his life to teaching until his passing at the age of 81 in 542 BCE. The Dharmachakra (eight-spoked wheel) represents the Four Noble truths and the Eightfold Path that the Buddha taught.

The Four Noble Truths

Suffering exists.
Suffering arises from attachment to desires.
Suffering ceases when attachment to desire ceases.
Freedom from suffering is possible by practicing the...

The Eightfold Path

Right View/Perspective,
Right Intention
Right Speech
Right Action
Right Livelihood
Right Effort
Right Mindfulness
Right Contemplation/Concentration

The time has come for you to let go of any belief that you are not worthy of love and affection. Love is all around you!!

*"You can search throughout the entire universe
for someone who is more deserving
of your love and affection than you are yourself,
and that person is not to be found anywhere.
You yourself, as much as anybody in the entire universe
deserve your love and affection."*
- Buddha -

33. Judaism - Throat

Judaism is a belief based in the ancient oral tradition of storytelling that began over 5000 years ago. "God" asked Abraham for obedience to him the One God. Monos is Greek for single; theos is Greek for God. Monotheism therefore means "One God". Through the lineage of Abraham, a mystical merchant from Sumeria (modern day Iraq), the foundation of Judaism, Christianity and Islam were formed. The Jewish or Hebrew people are seen as direct descendents of Isaac. Isaac is the Son of Abraham and Sarah who followed the voice of "God" as he promised to make Abraham the "Father of a Great Nation". Around 1400 BCE, "God" spoke to Moses, a descendent of Abraham and Isaac, to lead his people out of bondage in Egypt and into the "Promised Land." Moses never reached the Promised Land but he did receive the Ten Commandments along with instructions on how to build the Ark of the Covenent and the Menorah. All of this was given to him directly from the voice of "God".

Judah, the son of Jacob, Grandson to Isaac and Great Grandson to Abraham, claimed a large tract of land known as the land of Judah. In 1020 BCE, a young Hebrew warrior defeats Goliath and declares himself the first King of Israel. King David establishes Jerusalem as its capitol. His son King Solomon builds Solomon's Temple in 950 BCE. In 450 BCE the "Men of Great Assembly" known as the Sanhedrin officially commit the oral stories to paper and wrote the Torah. The first book of Genesis recounts the creation story, Noah and the great flood, plus the story of Abraham. In the creation story God creates the heavens and earth in six days. On the seventh day he rests, in Jewish tradition this is the Sabbath. Genesis also contains the story of Adam and Eve and the Garden of Eden where God commanded man to eat from any tree in the garden but not from the Tree of Knowledge of good and evil. God then created Eve as a helper for Adam and made her from his rib. A serpent encouraged Eve to eat of the Tree of Knowledge, saying, "when you eat from it your eyes will be opened and you will be like God, knowing good and evil." Eve ate the fruit and gave some to Adam who also ate it. Then their eyes were opened. Then God cursed the serpent and told Adam and Eve that from dust you were made and to dust you shall return. He banished them from the Garden of Eden and forbid them from ever eating of the Tree of Life and living forever. God separated man from their divinity and made them mortals on earth. The Star of David is a symbol based on the shape of King David's shield. The top triangle strives upward, toward God, while the lower triangle strives downward, toward earth. You are being reminded that you are from the heavens and the earth. It is time to speak your truth and share your gifts.

"Let us make man in our image,
after our likeness."
- Genesis 1:26 -

34. Christianity - Third Eye

Christianity is based on the teachings of Jesus, who encouraged people to see that the "Kingdom of God" was within them. Jesus was born into a Jewish family when Rome was in control of the Temple Mount in Jerusalem. The Romans worshipped the Sun as God, the Sol Invictus; they celebrated his birth on Dec. 25th, the Winter Solstice. Many Christians believe that Jesus was born through Immaculate Conception with the Virgin Mary. Her ancestry is related to Abraham, thereby preserving the "seed" and the direct connection to the "God" of Abraham. The Jewish books of the Old Testament are combined with the New Testament to create the Holy Bible. Jesus (Yeshua) of Nazareth is a Mystic, a Man and a Messiah the one and only Son of God. For this reason the faith that surrounds his teachings are vast and varied. Around 30 ACE Jesus chose John the Baptist to purify him with water as a rite of passage. After his baptism Jesus went on a fast in the mountains for 40 days and 40 nights.

When he returned he began to teach. His followers included fishermen, women, Samaritans and tax collectors. Jesus taught non-judgment, forgiveness, and compassion, which was in stark contrast to local Roman law and Jewish tradition. Many Jews were hoping for a Messiah who would reclaim the Temple Mount. Some were shocked by his interpretations of Jewish law, his power with people, and the belief that the Kingdom of God is within. Others called Jesus "King of the Jews"; this made Romans rulers and the Jewish orthodoxy uncomfortable. Jesus gave sermons in open fields and hillsides where people gathered to hear his mysterious parables. Jesus and his disciples traveled to Jerusalem for Passover, and shared a traditional Seder dinner. The next day Jesus was arrested for crimes against Rome. Jesus was brought before the Roman Prefect, Pontius Pilate who asked him if he was the King of the Jews. When Jesus replied, *"My kingdom is not of this world,"* Pilate condemned him to crucifixion. After Jesus' death Mary Magdalene and Mary, the mother of Jesus, prepared his body in Jewish tradition. A few days later Mary Magdalene experienced a vision of Jesus and shared this information with Peter and the other disciples. They began to argue over the interpretation of what Jesus said to her. The teachings of Jesus became convoluted and confused as Roman rulers persecuted early followers and then ultimately claimed this faith in 325 ACE. Look within for the answers you seek. Trusting your inner knowing to guide you from a place of love. See with your heart instead of your eyes.

"Why do you notice the splinter in your brothers eye,
but do not perceive the wooden beam in your own eye?
How can you say to your brother, Let me remove that splinter from
your eye, while the wooden beam is in your eye?
You hypocrite, remove the wooden beam from your eye first; then you
will see clearly to remove the splinter from your brothers eye."
- Matthew 7:3 -

35. Islam - Crown

Islam is inspired by a series of "Night Visits" from the Archangel Gabriel to Muhammad. Islam is the newest of the Abrahamic faiths with the belief in the One God of All (Allah). Ishmael and Isaac are sons of Abraham, both were told they would be Fathers of Great Nations. Ishmael is the elder son, born of Hagar. Muhammad, a descendent of Ishmael, was born in Mecca in 570 ACE. His father died before he was born, his mother, Amina, died when he was 6. Muhammad was in the care of his grandfather for two years, and then his uncle Abu Talib. Muhammad married Khadija who had children from a former marriage; she had 4-7 more children with Muhammad. Their oldest daughter was Fatima. The sacred Kaaba or God block was destroyed by fire in 605 ACE. Muhammad helped to rebuild it. He set the Black Stone onto a sheet and invited the chiefs of all the tribes in the city to lift the cloth together. He then placed the Black Stone in the East Corner, not knowing the direction his life would take.

Muhammad began receiving divine revelations in the form of dreams in 610 ACE. In each vision the Archangel Gabriel speaks for God and Muhammad begin reciting what he heard. Muhammad is accused of not respecting the religion of his forefathers. At the age of fortyone, Muhammad experiences his most profound "Night Journey". He was sleeping on a carpet when Gabriel invites Muhammad to ride on the back of the winged horse of Abraham called Burak. They fly over the Holy Lands of Moses and Jesus until they come to the Heavenly Lote Tree rooted in Jerusalem. Here Gabriel introduces him to angels and prophets. As he enters the 7th heaven, he sees a beautiful luminous tree with multi-colored leaves. It was in this tree that he learned of the universal spirit and divinity that is in everyone. It is here that he heard the original "purer" stories of Adam, Noah, Enoch, Abraham, Moses and Jesus. The Qur'an is created based on the recitation of the words Muhammad recieves from Gabriel. Muhammad is forced to leave Mecca and establishes Medina, "the city of the messenger". In 630 ACE Muhammad enters Mecca and cleanses the Kaaba of all previous idols. Muhammad instructs his followers to face Mecca five times a day for prayers and performs the Hajj or pilgrimage that honors the creation story and the lives of Abraham, Hager and Ishmael. Allah became the Supreme One Lord of the Kaaba. Muhammad died at the age of 62 in Medina, 632 ACE. His belief is called Islam his followers are called Muslims. Muslims see Muhammad as the last true prophet of God. His faith inspires us to follow our dreams. Dreams hold insights for your life. Journal your dreams whenever possible for you never know when your dreams will take flight. Writing them on paper is the first step to dreaming your world into being.

"None of you is a believer until you love for your brother what you love for yourself."
- Muhammad -

Consciousness

Awakening Within

Carl Jung's understanding of the development of consciousness provides a framework for how the archetype of the Tree of Life is held within our psyche. He saw that humans shared similar experiences or awareness even though they did not interact with each other. He called this the "collective unconscious." By awakening our collective unconsciousness we become conscious of the collective stories we hold. This gives us the unique ability to begin healing at the level of the sacred.

Roots of the tree - personal unconsciousness
Trunk of the tree – personal consciousness
Branches of the tree – collective unconsciousness
Tree as a whole – collective consciousness

We are all living trees of life!

Physically your legs and feet are your "roots" your torso is your "trunk" and your arms and head are your "branches." From this place imagine sending your roots to the deepest places within earth for nourishment as your arms reach for the highest dimensions in space. See that you are traveling through time and space yet standing in the present moment without judgment. Awaken within to feeling whole and loved.

*"One is wise to cultivate
the tree that bears fruit in our soul"
- Henry David Thoreau -*

36. Container of Life - Root

The Container of Life forms the foundation of your energy body. It connects you with the earth and all that the earth gives you. It is the sacred circle of creation, which represents a beginning that has no end. This sacred circle holds space for you to grow and reach your fullest potential as both human and divine. Many ancient sages saw the circle as the place of ultimate creation. Work with your Root Chakra as you visualize a container filled with rich dark soil that is fertilized with your loving intentions and actions. Know that this soil will also mulch the heavy energies and stories that no longer serve you. Build a loving and reciprocal relationship with the earth so you can energetically shed your wounds just as a serpent sheds its skin. Enjoy getting your hands dirty as you create a receptive and fertile foundation from which to grow. The time has come to start fresh. You have learned a great deal from the past and this has given you the ability to see what your heart truly desires. Begin to manifest your desire.

37. Portal of Life - Sacral

The Portal of Life represents your ability to create. It is located within your Sacral Chakra. This is where the essence of creation begins as two new cells emerge from the one. This division can also create judgment and a feeling of separation. Male and female are defined as separate yet they come together to create life. As the harmony of opposites plays out in your every day life, you are able to reveal and receive information that helps you feel balanced and whole. By understanding this dynamic flow you step out of judgment or feelings of separation. This is the creative process at work within you. It is important to see how opposites are necessary to create. Together they are whole and contain the dualities of life in all its perfection. The light and the dark co-exist in perfect harmony. The push and pull of life fuels your creative force. Embrace the energy of opposing forces within you. Release all expectations and judgment as you step into a time of co-creation within yourself and others.

38. Seed of Life - Solar Plexus

The Seed of Life is made up of six circles that have divided from the one. It is located within your Solar Plexus Chakra. It represents your inner courage and desire. This is also considered to be the seed of creation. The seventh circle in the center is your connection to source. This is the place of your intentions and the courage to manifest them. The seed of life is an idea you planted in your conscious or subconscious mind that is beginning to sprout. As you let your light shine you are able to nurture that which exists within you. The dreams you have been holding are about to blossom. The rumblings you are feeling are necessary for your inner awakening. Connect with the strength and wisdom within you and trust that you are being supported to make this happen. The sacred masculine within you provides the seed of desire and the sacred feminine nurtures this seed until you are ready to move forward. Fuel this growing passion within you by nurturing yourself with love and light.

39. Flower of Life - Heart

The Flower of Life contains the essence of your heart and soul. It represents pure love. It is the source of your life force energy. Your heart is opening and revealing the true essence of who you are. See your heart with new eyes as you share your essence with others. Imagine your self, as a flower that opens and closes at will. Be open during the day to gather and share love. At night allow your self to go within and recharge. Enjoy the dance of living between worlds. The Flower of Life is one of the oldest patterns on earth. This symbol was flash burned into the Osirian Temple and studied by Leonardo DaVinci. It is anchored in your heart yet it surrounds your entire energy field. Each dot within the Flower of Life can be seen as a portal that holds the same matrix. It is infinite and interconnected to all that is. By feeling the Flower of Life within, you can sense the infinite nature of your soul. By opening your heart you can see how the unconditional power of love ripples through life.

40. Fruit of Life - Throat

The Fruit of Life is associated with the Biblical story in the Garden of Eden. It is the divine fruit of immortality that was taken from Adam and Eve when they ate the forbidden fruit from the Tree of Knowledge. This epic story planted the seed of original sin that punishes mankind for seeking wisdom and speaking truth. The Fruit of Life is rooted in the Tree of Life. The Tree of Life represents our soul body while the Tree of Knowledge is our physical body. This one story separated man from his soul and has become etched in the collective unconsciousness of the Western Mind. The Fruit of Life is held in your Throat Chakra. It is time for you to reclaim the wisdom of your soul without fear. Your voice is your fruit, an expression of your gifts. Now is the time to heal the old stories of your life and create new ones. This will help you speak your truth from a place of peaceful power. Words spoken with love are gifts to the world. Use your words wisely as they are carried by the winds and scattered in all directions.

41. Knowledge of Life - Third Eye

The Knowledge of Life is revealed when the "feminine" circles of the Fruit of Life are connected within their core by "masculine" lines. By literally "connecting the dots" the circular and linear world come together as one. Both linear and circular are necessary to see the "whole" picture. From this place you can begin to sense your inner knowing, which stimulates your brain to awaken. The knowledge you have been seeking is now awakening within you. Trust in your knowing and awaken to the fact that you are both human and divine. The gift of being human is that you can see the divine within you. Use your knowledge wisely and what you seek will be revealed within your soul. When you fully awaken to your humananess and your divinity you will see that you are one within your self and your universe. This is what the great sages of the world have been teaching for thousands of years. Becoming conscious awakens your unconscious self, which in turn helps to awaken and heal the collective unconscious.

42. Star of Life - Crown

The Star of Life is also called the Merkaba (mer = light, ka = spirit, and ba = body). It is revealed within your Crown Chakra as you awaken your Third Eye. The Merkaba symbolizes the union of your divine soul with your human soul surrounded by counter-rotating wheels of light, "wheels within wheels", which transports your spirit from one dimension to another. The word Merkaba is an ancient Hebrew word for Chayot or "Chariot". This symbol reminds you that you are a spiritual being that is awakening to being both human and divine. Tear down any walls that separate you from that reality. Limiting beliefs do not serve you as you move forward and live with this new perspective. By awakening to the fact that you are a spiritual being having a human experience you are able to sense the infinite world within you. Begin to see the stars as your ancestors, or home away from home, supporting you on your journey. Sense the infinite nature of the universe that surrounds you and know that you are one and the same.

Soul
The Infinite One

Your soul creates the infinite "one" as the seven chakras within your energy body weave together into a multi-dimensional sphere. This sphere containing "wheels within wheels" the surrounds your entire being with energy that is anchored in your heart. From this place of the soul you can see that your chakras are unique yet also interrelated as they form the infinite one. From this place of oneness you are able to fully awaken to your true self-radiant nature. You are able to step out of ordinary reality and into non-ordinary reality where your spirit is free to travel through time and space. Seven is the organizing number that reveals the infinity symbol found in the number eight. It is no accident that the ancients organized our world in this way. Self-discovery encourages each of us to reclaim our unique spirit within.

Root – Muscular/Skeletal & Excretory System
Sacral – Reproductive System & Urinary System
Solar Plexus – Digestive, Lymphatic & Immune System
Heart – Circulatory & Respiratory System
Throat – Endocrine & Vocal System
Third Eye – Nervous & Sensory System
Crown – Belief System

*"Who looks outside dreams,
who looks inside awakes."
- Carl Jung -*

43. Soul Journey - Root

The Kabbalistic Tree of Life represents the journey of your soul as it manifests into human form and back into the unmanifested realm of the divine or Ein Sof "without end". The Tree of Life diagram is color coded to understand how it relates to your chakras. Each dot on the diagram is called a Sefirot (*) or emanation of divine will. The red dot correlates to the Root Chakra or the Sefirot Malkuth. To understand the Kabbalah "receiving/tradition" is to travel through the Tree of Life itself. The Kabbalalistic Tree of Life appears in the Flower of Life matrix or Heart Chakra. This sacred mystery teaching is also found in the construction of the Judaic seven-branched Menorah representing the seven lamps of the seven sages. These seven lamps are also known as the: Moon, Venus, Mercury, Sun, Jupiter, Mars, and Saturn. The central stem of the Menorah represents the trunk of the tree or spinal column where the masculine and feminine aspects of humanity come together to create the infinite, self-giving, radiant one.

The left three branches represent the sacred Feminine, or the Tree of Life. The right three branches are the sacred Masculine, or the Tree of Knowledge. Uriel, the Archangel or Serpent of Light is seen as the divine life force energy that helps man travel through the Tree of Life itself. Reincarnation of the soul to human form is a central theme in the Kabbalah.

1. Root Chakra - Red
*Malkuth - (1) - center, neutral
    Aspect - Kingdom, Physical, Sovereignty
    Angel - Sandalphon - Twin brother to Metatron
    Planet - Earth

2. Sacral Chakra - Orange
*Yesod - (2) center, neutral
    Aspect - Foundation
    Angel - Gabriel - Messenger of mercy and peace
    Planet - Moon

3. Solar Plexus Chakra - Yellow
*Hod - (3) - left, feminine
    Aspect - Splendor, Glory, Majesty
    Angel - Michael - Protector, defender of justice
    Planet - Mercury
*Netzach - (4) - right, masculine
    Aspect - Victory
    Angel - Haniel - Recovers lost secrets of healing
    Planet - Venus

4. Heart Chakra - Green
*Tiphereth - (5) - center, neutral
    Aspect - Beauty, Harmony
    Angel - Raphael - Healer of the human heart & body
    Cosmos - Sun

5. Throat Chakra – Blue
*Geburah - (6) - left, feminine
    Aspect - Intelligence, Strength, Severity
    Angel - Khamael - Protector of fear
    Planet - Mars
*Chesed - (7) - right, masculine
    Aspect - Mercy, Will, Loving Kindness, Greatness
    Angel - Zadkiel - Bringer of mercy and compassion
    Planet - Jupiter

6. Third Eye Chakra - Violet
*Binah - (8) - left, feminine
    Aspect - Intuition, Understanding - Mother
    Angel - Tzaphkiel - Defender of spiritual strife
    Planet - Saturn
*Chokhmah - (9) - right, masculine
    Aspect - Wisdom, Potential - Father
    Angel - Raziel - Keeper of secrets & divine wisdom
    Planet - Zodiac

7. Crown Chakra - White
*Kether - (10) -center, neutral
    Aspect - Throne, Crown, Above conscious will
    Angel - Metatron/Shekinah - Divine Scribe/Voice
    Planet - Space

8. Soul - Mystical State of Infinite Sharing - Grey
*Da'at - (enlightenment/oneness) - self-giving - united
    Angel - Elohim/Yahweh
    Planet - Sirius

You are entering a time of profound awakening as your soul is expanding its sense of awareness and purpose. It is vital to stay grounded and connected to the earth during this time.

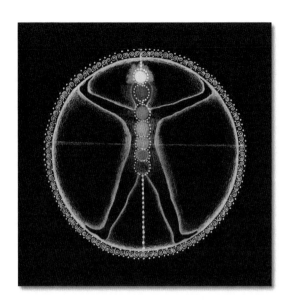

44. Soul Body - Sacral

You are a living breathing Tree of Life! Your legs and feet represent the roots, your torso represents the trunk and your arms, neck and head represents the branches. The left side of your body is representative of the sacred feminine and the right is your sacred masculine. Combining the energy of the feminine and masculine creates the two serpents of light or Kundalini Energy that swirls up your spinal column representing the trunk of the tree. This is your life force energy that is also seen as the two strands of your DNA. They hold your genetic code, and the ancestral records of your mother and fathers lineage. Your brain is divided between a left and a right hemisphere yet operates as one. Science has discovered that the right hemisphere of your brain (intuitive sacred feminine) controls the left side of your body. The left hemisphere (logical sacred masculine) controls the right side of your body. Oneness is achieved when you recognize that the masculine and feminine are balanced within you.

Two serpents of light can also be seen intertwined within the Caduceus, the symbol of modern medicine. The Gods Mercury and Hermes are seen as guides for the souls of man, they each carry a Caduceus in one arm. The rod is symbolic of the Tree of Life and your spinal column. When you see yourself as a Tree of Life you can connect to your true nature and trust your inner compass. Your soul serves as the guiding star that helps you navigates through life. The chakras of your Soul Body are associated with the eight directions.

Eight chakras and the eight sacred directions
1. **Root** - South
2. **Sacral** - West
3. **Solar Plexus** - North
4. **Heart** - East
5. **Throat** - Below
6. **Third Eye** - Center
7. **Crown** - Above
8. **Soul** - Around & Within

Now is a great time to understand where you are, where you have been and where you want to go. Allow yourself to feel grounded with the earth yet open to new adventures. Sense in your heart the direction your soul wants to take. This is an excellent time to rethink and shift your focus in a new direction. Remember that all possiblities are available to you.

45. Soul Spectrum - Solar Plexus

Enjoy all the colors of the universe including black. Bring something colorful into your life that speaks to your soul. Honor the darkness of night as well as the light of day by not taking it for granted. See them both as a gift that fuels you and nourishes you on the level of the soul. The Soul Spectrum manifests itself as an Aura that surrounds your entire energy body and is anchored in your heart. All colors found within the auric field are created by white light. Black is the absence of light. Our eyes can only see within the spectrum of visible white light. Black light produces ultra-violet light, which means "uber (above) violet" and is invisible to the human eye. What we see in black light bulbs is the violet glow created by phosphor, a substance that emits visible light in response to radiation, which is also light. UVA & UVB are two types of ultra-violet light also generated by the sun. The word phosphorus was created by the ancient Greeks to describe the planet Venus as the "light bearer" or morning star.

In Latin it also became known as Lucifer and was attributed to Venus as the evening star or "fallen angel". This mythology eventually became intertwined with the devil and darkness. They added fear to the stories of judgment between good and evil, light and dark etc...To embrace the full spectrum of who you are you must also embrace the darkness within you. The dark energy or dark matter is what holds your body together and provides the backdrop for all the colors of life to be revealed. If you are standing in a room of pure white light you will become "blinded". It is important to see the beauty of the dark energy that holds your soul as well as the light.

The colors of our energy body

1. Red: Is named after the life giving properties of blood. Red also represents honor, love and prosperity.

2. Orange: Is named after the color of a ripe orange.

3. Yellow: The word is historically associated with jaundice and cowardice. Yet the color of our sun, our power source is yellow.

4. Green: Is named after the German word, grow.

5. Blue: Is related to the concept of bright and shiny.

6. Violet: Is another name for purple. Purple originated as a Greek word to describe the color created by the spiny dye-murex snail.

7. White: Is a word derived from the word for "light" or bright". The Sun, the Moon and the Stars are the sources of natural light.

8. Black: Is the absence of visible light yet it makes up the majority of matter in the universe. Black is the color that holds us together in both human and divine form.

Bring color into your life in a new way. Open yourself up to explore and feel all the colors available to you and try them on. Apply this to what you wear, eat, enjoy, and feel.

46. Soul Essence - Heart

Flowers remind you to breathe in the beauty of the essential nature of who you are and who you want to be. See your soul as a flower and the beauty and potential within it. Your seven primary chakras come together to form an infinite soul anchored in your heart. Oneness occurs in the Awakened Heart where the Tree of Knowledge and the Tree of Life are one. Together they create the Flower of Life matrix that contains your Soul's Essence. This essence is the love you share with the world. Scientists have proven that our heart is the electromagnetic core of our being, this core is connected to the core of our earth and all that live upon it. Our actions create reactions. Our essential nature is to share with others. Our soul essence is our greatest gift. It transcends ordinary reality and connects with others on the level of the soul. Together we can support each other in realizing that we live in the Garden of Eden here on Earth. Let us treasure it and nurture it every moment we have in this lifetime...

Trees unconditionally offered life-giving wood for fire, shelter plus fruits, nuts, sap (maana). Most importantly they show man how to live in harmony with the natural cycles of life.

Spring - Birth - East - Sun Rise - Morning - Trees blossom
Summer - Life - South - Sun Above - Daytime - Trees fruit
Fall - Death - West - Sun Set - Evening - Trees release
Winter - Rebirth - North - Sun Below - Night - Trees recharge

The Celtic Calendar is representative of the cycles of the seasons and the desire of your soul to connect with nature.

The Celtic Calendar based on the Solar Year

East - Spring Equinox - Sun Rising - Birth - A Time to Birth
SE - Beltane - Festival of Beltane - A Time to Blossom
South - Summer Solstice - Sun Above - Life - A Time of Love
SW - Lammas - Festival of First Harvest - A Time to Bake
West - Fall Equinox - Sun Setting - Death - A Time to Release
NW - Samhain - Festival of the Dead - A Time to Honor
North - Winter Solstice - Sun Below - Rebirth - A Time Within
NE - Imbolc - Festival of Brigid – A Time to Bring Light

Your soul is coming full circle as it is connecting with the cycles of the seasons. Look at your life as if you were a tree and ask yourself what season are you in? Does the season you feel match up to the actual season of the year? If not it is time to help your soul get in sync with the seasons. This will help you in all areas of your life. As your soul connects with the cycles of nature you will begin to feel more comfortable in your body and with the world around you. Life will become easier as you see how the outer world is reflected within you. Embrace the essence of your soul as you release, renew, rebirth and rejoice in the life you are creating!

47. Soul Sound - Throat

Sound is a powerful tool especially when it comes from a sacred place within you. You can create sound through chanting, drumming, singing or speaking. Tools such as singing bowls or tuning forks may be helpful. Take time to listen to the sounds in your life. Appreciate the sounds of nature and feel how it can help you heal and open your soul. Study the science and art of cymatics or join a drumming circle. Create a mantra that resonates with your soul. Whatever you choose do it with the intention of using sound to help you speak your truth and create a more loving world. Cultures around the world use sound to transform consciousness. Sound is vibrational in nature, and we are vibrational beings. Create a sound that resonates within your soul. Modern science now shows us that all life is vibrational in nature. The Sri Yantra is a depiction of the vibrational essence of creation, also called the mother of all yantras in Hindu tradition.

A Yantra is the physical form of a Mantra or prayer. Yantras are also Mandalas. The Sri Yantra represents the sound of awakening the creative life force energy within us. It is a created by nine intersecting triangles centered on the bindu point (the central point of the yantra). The five downward pointing triangles, represent Shakti; female life force energy. The four upright triangles, represent Shiva; male life force energy. Together they form harmony and expansion through the Mantra AUM. The Sri Yantra becomes a living symbol within you when the six chakras awaken through the Kundalini Shakti energy at the base of the spine, ascending through each of the chakras to the crown chakra. At this point, you transcend the symbol and awakened to your true nature as both male and female. This realization of the inner human journey is the awakening of your divinity. The circular letter "O" is directly related to the mantra of "Aum" which when toned or chanted represents our eternal connection to creation. It connects you to your own circular nature and that of the ever-evolving universe.

Seven notes and mantras within the energy body
1. **Root: Musical Note:** C   **Mantra:** LAM
2. **Sacral: Musical Note:** D   **Mantra:** VAM
3. **Solar Plexus: Musical Note:** E   **Mantra:** RAM
4. **Heart: Musical Note:** F   **Mantra:** YAM
5. **Throat: Musical Note:** G   **Mantra:** HAM
6. **Third Eye: Musical Note:** A   **Mantra:** AUM
7. **Crown: Musical Note:** B   **Mantra:** AH
8. **Soul Note**: Harmonic Convergence   **Mantra:** Silence

Each chakra within your body resonates to one of these seven primary notes of the musical scale as well as a unique mantra. Awaken within by realizing that pure vibration is the sound of your soul. Find your voice and let it be heard and honored.

48. Soul Tree - Third Eye

By reclaiming your soul as being both the Tree of Knowledge and the Tree of Life you see that good versus evil is just another story. By seeing how these stories hold insights and gifts for humanity we become more compassionate and whole. From this place we can see that we are human and we are learning. To awaken within is to accept the opportunities we have for learning from each other. Living from the place of the awakened soul brings true knowledge that empowers you to live with peace and love. Release all fear of being judged and all desire to judge others. Remind your self that everyone wishes to heal and live in peace and feel loved. The Soul Tree is nourished by the energy of all seven chakras flowing together, just like your soul body. Seven is the sacred number that is woven into the very fabric of your soul's story. The seven planets seen with the naked eye inspired the western mind to create divine order and epic stories. You are a Soul Tree. Now is the time for you to weave your epic story.

Seven Sages - Seven Lamps - Seven Days - Seven Planets

Sunday - Sun's Day (Sun)

Named for the Germanic Sun Goddess Sunna and the Roman day of Sol Invictus.   Other Sun Gods are Ra (Egyptian), Mithras (Roman/Persian/Hindu). The Sun rises in the East, the Germanic Goddess Eostre is the Spring Goddess of the East.

Monday - Moon's Day (Moon)

Named for the Germanic Moon God Mani, Sunna's Brother and the Roman day of Lunae or the Goddess Luna. Other names are Diana and Selene. The Egyptians saw the Moon as the seed that impregnated the Earth who then gave birth to a new Sun. Sin (Nanna) is the Arabian Moon God.

Tuesday - Tyr's Day (Mars)

Named for Tyr the Norse God of War and Law and the Roman day of Mars. Mars is God of War. Tyr is the son of Odin also known as Woden/Irmin/Yggr.

Wednesday - Wodan's Day (Mercury)

Named for the Norse God Wodan also known as Odin, Irmin and Yggr, the Father of all Gods and the Roman day of Mercury. Mercury leads souls between Heaven and Earth. Also known as Hermes (Greek), Thoth (Egyptian), Adonai (Chaldean), YWHW (Judaic), God (Christian), Allah (Islam).

Thursday - Thor's Day (Jupiter)

Named for the Norse God Thor, son of Odin and the Roman day of Jupiter. Jupiter is also the Greek God Zeus, son of Cronus. Zeus and Thor are both seen as protector Gods.

Friday - Freya's Day (Venus)

Named for Freya the Germanic and Norse Goddess of love and Roman day of Venus. Venus is the evening star. The Mother God known as Astarte, Asherah, Aphrodite, Eostre, Minerva, Innana, Alluza, Athena, etc...

Saturday - Saturn's Day (Saturn)

Named for the Roman day of Saturn or Cronus, Son of Uranus (Sky God) and Gaia (Earth Goddess).

49. Soul Light - Crown

Let your light shine for all to see. The time has come to stop hiding from yourself or hiding yourself from others. Love your self and radiate love. Know it is infinite. The Soul Light reflects your unique spirit. From this place imagine that you are a Soul of Light that is interconnected with everything in the universe. Feel your spirit beating in harmony with infinity. Sense how you are of the earth and of the universe. Many indigenous cultures believe that the Tree of Life is the Axis Mundi that runs through the center of our Milky Way galaxy. This tree anchors your soul to the core of the universe, reminding you that you come from the stars. When you awaken within you can imagine yourself as being in the center of the universe right here on earth. The Soul of Light occurs when you become the infinite one.

"As we let our own light shine,
we unconsciously give other people
permission to do the same."
- Nelson Mandela -

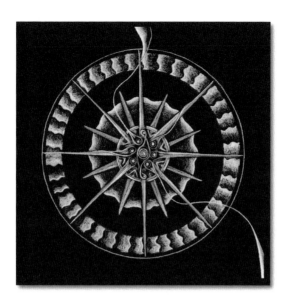

50. Ignition

It is time to jump-start your journey! See this mandala as a spark of pure energy that you can call on to energize your soul. Your subtle energy body holds your energetic/divine blueprint just as your DNA holds your physical blueprint. It vibrates at a very unique frequency and is in constant motion. The central "awakening spiral" is representative of your source, which is anchored in your Soul. The Golden spokes are interrelated with the Blue spokes. They are the masculine and feminine energy working together to create balance and movement. The oscillating vibrating wheels seen in this mandala are indicative of your energy body. The black spaces can be called the space "in between" that allows your Soul to travel through time and space to your source. When your soul is called back into human form the individual chakras begin to create luminous threads that ignite the human soul and anchors it into the physical body. Your first breath is your awakening call. Listen to what it is saying to you.

*"To see a world in a grain of sand
and heaven in a wild flower.
Hold infinity in the palms of your hand
and eternity in an hour."*
- William Blake -

51. Infinity

By twisting a circle 180° you create the symbol for infinity, which is also the shape of the number eight. When eight is divided by two you get four, which represents both your earthly and divine foundation. They are anchored in the midpoint, the place where your heart and soul intersect. The infinity symbol reflects the inner and outer journey of your infinite soul. This symbol is also reflective of your chakras. The lower loop or circle holds your Root, Sacral and Solar Plexus Chakra; the upper loop holds your Throat, Third Eye and Crown Chakra. The Heart Chakra is shared by both and serves as the gateway between worlds. The silver represents the sacred feminine and the gold represents the sacred masculine. The silver and gold travel in and around, this is symbolic of the lunar cycles of a 13 full moon (male) year and a 13 new moon (female) year. This is directly related to the Seed of Life and the Fruit of Life. Honor your infinite nature as you create new opportunities and bring them to fruition.

*"Your inner purpose is to awaken. It is as simple as that.
You share that purpose with every other person on the planet-
because that is the purpose of humanity."*
- Eckhart Tolle -

Awakening the Mandalachakra™

The awakening spiral is one of the earliest expressions of higher consciousness. It is symbolic of the natural laws of order, beauty and symmetry. Leonardo Fibonacci, (1170 – 1250) an Italian mathematician discovered its numerical sequence by adding the previous two numbers together to form the next and so on and so on (1, 1, 2, 3, 5, 8, 13, 21, 34, 55...). He realized that you can divide any number in the sequence by the one before it and the answer is always close to 1.6180339887...this is known as the Golden Ratio, Golden Number or Golden Mean.

The awakening spiral is symbol found on the back of each Awaken Within card. This is symbolic of the Mandalachakra.

Another expression of numerical infinity is found in the concept of Pi. Pi is a mathematical constant that is the ratio odf a circle's circumference to its diameter. It is approximately equal to 3.14159. It is called an irrational number because its decimal representation never ends and never settles into a permanent repeating pattern. It is often called a transcendental number as it is impossible to square a circle with a compass and straight edge. This is why the circle itself is seen as a symbol of infinite potential and creation.

Resources

Banzhaf, Hajo & Theler, Brigitte. (2000) *Tarot and the Journey of the Hero*: Samuel Webster; Red Wheel/Weiser.

Campbell, Joseph. (1983) *The Way of the Power Animals, Volume 1. Historical Atlas of World Mythology.* New York: Harper Row

Cornell, Judith. (2006) *MANDALA: Luminous Symbols for Healing.* Adyar, India: Quest Books, Theosophical Publishing.

Cornell, Judith. (1997) *Drawing the Light from Within*: Adyar, India: Quest Books, Theosophical Publishing House.

Eisler, Riane. (1998) *Chalice and the Blade, Our History, Our Future:* New York, Harper Collins

Jung, C. G. (1968) *Man and his Symbols*: New York, Dell.

Sams, Jamie. (1999) *Dancing the Dream - The seven sacred paths of human transformation:* San Francisco, HarperCollins.

Villoldo, Alberto. (2006) *The Four Insights:* Carlsbad, California: Hay House, Inc.

Villoldo, Alberto. (2000) *Shaman, Healer, Sage*: New York, New York, Harmony Books.

Wauters, Ambika. (2002) *The Book of Chakras – Discover the hidden forces within you:* London: Quarto Publishing.

White, Ruth. (1998) *Using your Chakras –A new approach to healing your life*: Barnes and Noble with Red Wheel/Weiser

Notes

Notes

18517698R00059

Made in the USA
Charleston, SC
07 April 2013